Carmella Natale

Lady Carmella's Love Weight Game

By: Carmella Natale

Carmella Natale

© 2014. Carmella Natale. All Rights Reserved.
Boss Lady Enterprise Publishing, LLC

Carmella Natale

Table of Contents

Prologue

Chapter 1: Introduction

Chapter 2: The Game

Chapter 3: Peace & Love

Chapter 4: Harmony

Chapter 5: Truth

Chapter 6: Faith

Chapter 7: Hope

Chapter 8: Light

Chapter 9: Joy

Chapter 10: Comfort

Chapter 11: Understanding

Chapter 12: Service

Chapter 13: Forgiveness

Chapter 14: Awakening

Chapter 15: Apply Psalm 91 and Transform Guilt

Carmella Natale

Prologue

When we are One with The One—God's Love, we inevitably win and triumph. This book is the story of Carmella Natale's victory of reaching her ideal weight. It is written to express God's love and to create hope and promise of success to fellow strugglers on life's highway, especially those who are struggling with the issue of correct body weight.

Carmella Natale

Chapter 1: Introduction

When I moved to Dallas and began my career, life looked prosperous and full of hope. Because I was well placed in terms of family, financial wealth and general well-being, I was accepted in the best circles of influence and with individuals in the inner circle of professional football players and celebrities in the area. Yet, with all of these blessings and advantages I still felt emptiness and lack.

Thanksgiving and Christmas dinners were lavish and physically filling, but could not satisfy me on the inside. A gnawing feeling and sense of lack of fulfillment tugged my inner soul, and my life reached an unavoidable crisis point while I waited at Dallas Love Field for my return to Amarillo, Texas. I felt desperate as I staggered to pay a phone wanting, but unable to tell my family about my hopelessness. All flights were grounded because of a storm, but I didn't want to go back nor live anymore anyway. Yet and still, I didn't want to die.

"What are you going to do, Lady?" I asked myself, out loud, slurring the words. I opened the phone book to restaurants and called the one that had the greatest influence on me from the page, IL Sorrento.

"Is the Owner there? May I speak to him please?" As soon as he was on the line words tumbled out of my mouth.

"Would you like to add flair to your experiences for your customers?" I asked

"And what would that be?" he replied

"A metaphysical reader." I responded with confidence.

"Start tomorrow evening." The owner demanded

"I'll be there two weeks from tomorrow evening." I retorted. I knew immediately that we'd love each other's strong personalities and we did.

I had no idea what to do for two weeks, but I stood by my word and showed up, sober as a metaphysical reader. The customers loved me and were amazed that I knew so much about them! In two days, I was offered a place to live at the Preston Towers in the uptown area of Dallas. From here, I could walk across the street to the restaurant where I worked, and for years I resided in the same apartment even after IL Sorrento closed.

Meanwhile, I lost about a hundred pounds, not by eating at the restaurant, but by embracing the fullness of God's love as I worked, lived, and learned to love myself in this wonderful part of Dallas.

CHANGE YOUR WEIGHT THROUGH LOVE

Please understand that I have not set myself up as knowing all the answers to spiritual Love, or even as a teacher. I am a teacher because we're all teachers, and teaching all of the time. We're teachers by the way we treat our fellow man and by how we walk among them. I'm communicating my message from the basis of the fact that I have changed my life by applying what I know about spirituality and the laws of Love.

By having this Light in me, I ache for my fellow men that haven't seen and don't have this Light. God's thoughts speak to us all day long. The Voice is always soothing and one of joy. Joy is the only real feeling we have. Happiness is the knowledge that we are love, that we have love, and that we give love. Unhappiness is a state of aching for love and the knowing or sensing that we don't have it, can't give it, or receive it. As a student of **A Course in Miracles**, I've learned and do realize that ALL is Love, and the rest is illusion. From this premise, we'll look at our relationship with ourselves and our relationship with God.

A LOVE STORY

Habits, addictions, and compulsions are calls for help. We are looking for peace and to feel safe. Feeling safe allowed me to give up my addiction to prescription drugs and get acquainted with the REAL me. Then, I was able to have companionship with REAL me.

We all know that diets don't work. What does "diet" mean? The first three letters spell, "DIE". It doesn't mean victory; it means "die"! We've all tried to diet over and over again, and have failed again and again. Now, we're going to play the game, have fun, and win. We'll be winners in more ways than one.

This approach to your life will be a love story. It will be the story God meant for it to be bringing joy to your heart and Light to your path. Thus, the path is clear of darkness, and Love will be your Light and protection.

Carmella Natale

Chapter 2: The Game

Let's have fun—let's get started. By now you know that by being Love, we conquer. Love reforms us into a new person, a new "me" or "I". We will no longer attribute power to our bodies and feel victimized by the illusion that our bodies have power over us.

Self-deception is a basic aspect of being in our illusory world of perception. Our ears, for example, hear what we desire for them to hear. Guilt is also a basic and prevalent experience for us. In order to alter our perception of this experience, self-discipline is needed and this discipline changes our operation from our false self into our REAL self. If we have been living in guilt, the change to self-acceptance can be and usually is difficult for many. The rewards, including loss of excess body weight, are what make this transition worthwhile.

St. Francis of Assisi is one of history's most admired and revered champions of mental discipline. For this reason, I choose him and his famous prayer as the guide for disciplining our minds. St. Francis showed us how to grow spiritually through avoidance of selfishness and overindulgence in the physical senses. As we follow his guidance through his awesome prayer, we will be able to focus our minds on health, wholeness, and happiness. This state of genuine love for our REAL self will automatically regulate our physical body to its ideal state. Meditate upon the idea of *loss of false self leads to loss of excess weight*. The "false self", (the ego) will resist, struggle and even scream because it wants the attention and wants to survive. When we are seriously playing the Love Weight Loss Game, the ego will strike back by attempting to attack or defeat us at every turn. The prayer of St. Francis will show us how to change our attitude from the false sense of selfishness, to the truth of caring. This prayer will show us how to disrobe and let go of the "false costumes" we've also been wearing.

We're beginning to increase awareness that it's healthy to let go of mental baggage. I smile as I remember once giving eight bags of clothing to Goodwill, and letting go of so much mental baggage, while learning to love. You can perceive that we must dig deeper and operate at a more serious level than the usual cliché's and conversations to which we've become accustomed. Instead of surface explorations, we're involved in learning how to love with our whole soul, whole mind, and whole body. We risk hurting ourselves more with aborted attempts at growth because this process requires forward progress without return or retreat.

The Love Game and is not about getting, taking, or acquiring; it's about clearing, cleaning, and undoing. It's the process of cleansing our minds of negative thoughts and beliefs. In addition to this, it clears our cells of toxins and excess energies of any kind. It's letting go of negative mental baggage, and expressing our inherent love and joyousness instead. We will begin to wear new clothes of forgiveness. The effects of this process will allow us to love ourselves and loose our fear of the reactions of others by confronting us with the "false costumes" we're wearing today also known as "our extra weight".

THE PRAYER OF ST. FRANCIS OF ASSISI

"Lord, make me an instrument of Thy peace,

That where there is hatred, I may bring love,

That where there is discord, I may bring harmony,

That where there is error, I may bring truth,

That where there is doubt, I may bring faith,

That where there is despair, I may bring hope,

That where there are shadows, I may bring light,

That where there is sadness, I may bring joy.

Lord, grant that I may seek rather more to comfort than to be comforted,

More to understand than to be understood,

More to love, than to be loved.

For it is by self-forgetting one finds love.

It is by forgiving that one is forgiven.

It is by dying that one awakens to Eternal Life. Amen"

Carmella Natale

Chapter 3: Peace and Love

"Lord, make me an instrument of thy peace."

Love equals peace. The Charming Woman accepts God's endowment of dominion and learns how to express it lovingly in all situations and circumstances. As peace is claimed within, physical cravings diminish. Love fills the emptiness and satisfies the "hunger". Thus God's Love equals peace. A piece of cake or a hearty serving of candy can actually stimulate cravings for more, but the need for "more" separates us from enough. Love fills the void created by feeling empty and the disciplines of gratitude, courtesy and respect are our friends.

> Gratitude—Expressing thanks for blessings and satisfactions already present, and for challenges which will lead to growth. This replaces "stuffing the self" in an effort to reduce or stop cravings.

> Courtesy—Interpreting situations that involve hunger with kindness rather than negativity.

> Respect—Accepting and allowing praise and positive emotions

Compliment any cooperation. Create space for love, and see forgiveness rather than guilt and punishment. Inaccurate interpretations are the attacks of the ego. Break the habit of blame.

Get out of guilt, self-hatred, and attacks of the false self. Come to an awareness of action, and declare ownership of all that is yours.

LOVE

That where there is hatred, I may bring love."

    The charming woman diminishes and finally dissolves the fear based false self. She perceives that peace and love are possible when she pauses, and chooses to express the REAL self instead of the false one.

    When people think we have our lives together, they don't nurture us. Personally, I'd rather talk to someone who has had and overcome the experiences that I have lived through. Separation keeps us isolated. Self-righteousness is another form of fear.

    We hurt so much that we do not think of asking for love. We're unaware of how to live in the world, so we confine ourselves to our own little circle. We must learn to see past our sense of never having enough, also known as lack. We gain weight, guilt, and self-hatred separating ourselves from God's love. When we put away ignorance, then we realize His Presence and lose our false self as we accept our REAL self as our identity.

    The Law of Love dictates that, "We shall have no other Gods before the Divine or Supreme Being of all there is." Since the kingdom of God is within us, and we're made in God's image and likeness, it follows that the Law of Love truly dictates "We shall have no other Gods before us." Understand that only the Divine and Supreme Being of all there is can wake us up every morning, and no matter how hard we try, we cannot stop our own hearts from beating. It is this absolute truth that solidifies the existence of a greater God that is living in each one of us and Whom is responsible for every GOOD deed or act we do. There's only one True Power and that is learning to love and live from the Internal Power within us. The First Commandment is the acceptance of the only Power there is. There's nothing else but illusions, they are what seem to be real. Let go of any fear we have in sickness, mental illness, addictions and so forth. The results of these fears bring forth the Law of Cause & Effect.

Only love is real and is a fact. Illusions of love are very deceptive and will eventually disappoint us. Yield to nothing that is outside of love. For God is love. Every miracle is letting go of the ego. Guilt always demands illusion and wants punishment in any form. The result is pain, depressions, fear, etc. There's no peace where love is not. Living from the false self we are constantly attacked by guilt and trapped by what our bodies want. Without guilt, there is no addiction, and guilt is more of our problem than fat. The choices we make are our problem. We choose the drug we want to keep.

Realizing I am already free from this compulsion of overeating, I am hearing more and more about how love gave us the freedom we all need. Here's where our soil needs cultivating. Life is lived from within, and whatever we plant grows.

Love can prevent and heal all wounds. Perfect love is always available but we resist and avoid it. The hunger for love persists until we allow it and accept its completion and fulfillment. "We are as God created us," which means that we were created as love. Our task is to accept the way we were created by disallowing the fears and limitations we've made instead. The connection between weight loss and love is here seen clearly and totally. We can love ourselves into our ideal body weight with the natural beauty of the Creator revealed in our physical form. Negative thoughts will lead in the opposite direction. Choose the path of love and enjoy life.

St. Francis taught and practiced the principle of being the loved and loving self. He placed emphasis on being full of love, sharing, and projecting it outwards to our brothers and sisters in humanity. Expansion is the nature of love, and to expand we must have love available.

Since God is love, love is one of the most common subjects among all human beings. History is full of efforts to write about it and express it in writing. The Apostle Paul achieved one of the most famous and powerful written forms about love in 1 Corinthians 13.

"If I had the gift of being able to speak in other languages without learning them, can could speak ever language there is in all of heaven and earth, but didn't love others, I would only be making noise. If I had the gift prophecy and knew all about what is going to happen in the future, knew everything about everything, but didn't love others what good would it do? Even if I had the gift of faith so that I could speak to a mountain and make it move, I would still be worth nothing at all without love. If I gave everything I have to poor people, and if I were burned alive for preaching the Gospel but didn't love others, it would be of no value whatever.

Love is patient and kind, never jealous or envious, never haughty, selfish, or rude. Love does not demand its own way. It is not irritable or touchy. It does not hold grudges and will hardly even notice when others do wrong. It is never glad about injustice, but rejoices when truth wins out. If you love someone you will be loyal to him no matter what the cost. You will always believe in him, always expect the best of him, and always stand your ground defending him. All the special gifts and powers from God will someday come to an end, but love goes on forever."

Paul concludes his famous treatise on love by presenting the value of the temporary nature of our spiritual gifts and powers and the contrast with the eternal nature and power of love. He closes with his immortal statement: "There are three things that remain—faith, hope, and love. The greatest of these is love."

You don't have to search for love because perfect love is already within you. You merely have to remove the barriers you have erected against it. Here is another very powerful idea. There are two forms of human behavior; expressions of love and requests for love. Overeating and eating incorrectly are requests for love rather than expressions of love.

When we apply all of these principles to the goal of ideal weight, we only become victorious. St. Francis lived by the principle of loving himself and everyone. We remember him especially for loving and respecting the poor and lepers of his day. St. Francis supports the idea that we are already perfect love and that we need to live from that premise rather than "needing to be loved", or having to make requests for love. Incorrect eating is a request for love and an attempt to answer the request with a substitute for love.

We can say that our first connection to love in our lives is the connection of the umbilical cord to the fetus by which we are nurtured for the first nine months of the body's existence. Mother's warmth and nurturance equals the definition of love. Immediately upon arrival in Mother Earth's atmosphere, a first goal is usually the first meal which is a connection to the Mother's breast. Love equals satisfaction at all levels through that experience and continues indefinitely...until weaning.

Love, nutrition, happiness and peace are so basic and interwoven that the world's history is full of study and literature on the subject. We know that learning through contrast is basic to being human so our history is full of contrasts about love versus fear, hate, anxiety, and deprivations of love and food.

The Spitz children of World War II are one of the most well known and most famous demonstrations of the contrasts between met and unmet needs. The Spitz children in the nursery were physically well cared for as all their physical needs were well met by good, trained people. The infants received their meals on time with food of good quality, and well prepared. Their diapers were changed promptly and regularly, yet with all these things done well the children all died. Later, it was understood that their needs for being loved, cared for, held, and treated as persons were not met, and because of it they left their bodies. The principle that proper maternal care leads to improved mental health and nutrition which leads to hearty and healthy infants is affirmed here as a principle for our babies today. Lessons can be learned from deprivation which can service as a motivator for life to be better and spur to greater achievements. The best norm for humanities evolution is the quality care, love, and the best quality nutrition which is also the preferred way.

The Japanese numbers are especially vital and important. The centenarians of Okinawa have become well known and inspiring due to their freedom from chronic diseases. These individuals whom live who live to or beyond the age of a hundred years live active and productive lives remaining very present until death or just a few months before. They're being studied so that we may know the secrets of the Okinawa centenarians.

Obvious factors in their success are genetics, little stress, exercise, and community love based on sharing activities and goals with others. Their diets consist of fresh organic vegetables, grains with rice, coral calcium and fish, and fruits from their own trees or self-harvested. One ninety-one year old lady is famous for climbing the trees and harvesting the fruit. Nature and balance, lack of chemicals, uncontaminated water, and other factors has made the centenarians of Okinawa. The truth they have come to know and experience has made them free, and if ever tempted they discerned the error choosing truth instead. Thus, the love of St. Francis and the devotion to truth have given the Earth the great gifts of the healthy lives of the Okinawans.

In conclusion of our study of love, it was the power of love for me that I was able to lose a hundred pounds and transform my personal life, develop my career in the restaurant as a reader, and enjoy every day as "the first day of the rest of my life". It was through the same power of love that I was able to build Natale's Italian Food and maintain it for ten years. My restaurant was voted the best of its kind by the Dallas Morning News and received many other honors because it was an environment where love of others was always present. If you put love into your business and life, without a doubt it'll flourish.

Loved and valued reader, you can have for yourself what you desire and long to achieve. Love yourself, love others, and the results will follow. There are endless books now, and the internet is full of diets and other weight loss methods. In the end, all of these may fail or be worth little, without love for yourself and others.

Chapter 4: Harmony

"That where there is discord I may bring harmony."

    The charming woman is in tune with the REAL self. She senses and hears the disharmony of guilt, and is aware of the potential harm in a single judgmental thought against herself. She also knows that it is equally harmful to project the attack of judgment upon any fellow humans. Disharmony follows all judgmental decisions. The actions and the hurt that linger after judgment are a result. Imbalances in the emotional body can result from these judgmental self-attacks. Actual physical weight gains can begin, and accelerate or become out of control. Occasionally we hear of someone who weighs 1,000 pounds. Several cases are now on record and have become highly visible to the media and public.

    The beautiful, legendary life of St. Francis is famous for the many conflicts which he transformed into harmony by practicing love for everyone and every creation of God. People loved and followed his ways of living, and because of this he was very powerful, loved, and respected in Rome. Because St. Francis lived his aforementioned prayer and walked his talk; the effect was that he was soon famous and well known throughout the world. His memory still lives on today and his love, peacemaking and harmonic presence during conflicts will remain in our hearts and minds for centuries to come.

One of the oldest and most famous cathedrals in America is a main feature of downtown Santa Fe, New Mexico. It is a place of beauty in terms of location, architecture, the beautiful, majestic trees in the park on the north side, and you can almost hear his voice speaking his prayer if you listen very carefully. This building is named in memory of the honorable life of St. Francis, and vibrations of harmony and peace have touched the endless people whom have visited the marvelous cathedral since 1600. In addition, one of the major streets in Santa Fe is St. Francis Avenue.

It may seem to be a long distance between St. Francis and weight loss, but there is no distance if the relationship between love for oneself, normal weight, physical health, and attractiveness are all understood. The infinitely well-known Louise Hay asserts that a major cause of excessive weight is "self-protection". In her best-selling book, <u>You Can Heal Your Life</u>, she describes brilliantly how fear, insecurity, self-criticism, and fear of criticism form the foundation for using food as a substitute for genuinely loving oneself. St. Francis lived and taught the total importance and necessity for loving ourselves, loving others, and avoiding all disharmony.

All negative emotions create imbalances in the emotional body. Pain has to be present and involved. Food has been the "drug of choice" for millions of humans as a way to reduce or deny pain. Thus it is true that we can change our weight through love. A simple guideline is, the more we love ourselves, the healthier our diets and lifestyles will become.

Decide now to love yourself unconditionally. Let this decision be your goal until it is achieved and let it be your main assistant along the challenging road to ideal weight.

Chapter 5: Truth

"That where there is error, I may bring truth"

Perfect body weight is an area where the discernment of error and truth is challenging. One reason for this challenge is the profit motive. Apparently there are individuals who will make, market, and sell anything that others will buy and eat regardless of the damage it may do. Fortunately, we can know the truth, and the truth will set us free.

Currently in America, truth is abounding as tremendous efforts are being made to have natural, organic fruits, vegetables and other foods available to us in endless supply. A major error creating worldwide distraction is encouraging customers to prefer or choose refined flours, sugars, and other chemically laden substances and products which fail to meet the standards of nature and truth. Love for ourselves and nature in conjunction with discernment of what will and will not hurt us will result in optimum health and avoid disease and illness.

There are cultures on Earth where a majority of people live on principles of love and truth averaging a lifespan of 125 years. In the Land of Hunza, for example, the people live peaceful lives and their diet is as natural, raw and as fresh as possible.

~~~~~~~~~~~~~~~~~~~~

Once upon a time, one Hunzukut killed another Hunzukut only to leave the whole culture stunned. The Elders had didn't know how to respond because it was a first time ever occurrence. They went into meditation and conference for a week to decide what to do with the one who took the life of a fellow human. After deliberating, they decided to send him out of the country forever from all he had and had known.

Here are some principles of the Hunza culture:
- Children breast feed until the age of three
- Adult diet features fresh fruits
- Apricot trees are the most desired inheritance from one's parents
- Love, respect for others, and respect for property are prime permanent values
- They are at peace with each other and their neighbors
- The men of Hunza are internationally famous for running hundreds miles per day at advanced ages with plenty energy.

Hunzaland is a great model for all of us to follow in terms of health and creative lives rooted in love and respect.

Art Linkletter made Hunza famous in the middle of the last century. He financed a research journey for an individual to live in Hunza culture for a short amount of time. This man returned to America with his findings in writing to make an appearance on Art Linkletter's show. The man described the Hunza as being a remarkable people with excellent health and lifestyles. Ever since the show, the Hunza have been well known and famous for their peaceful and quality existence.

The studies of aging and anti-aging have multiplied since that period of time. Centenarians, who are individuals living to or beyond the age of one hundred, have increased in number and will continue to increase dramatically. Concerns are rising that this may be a partial cause for overpopulation; however, there is no need for us to live in any form of fear.

A brief look at current statistics for centenarians on Earth reveals much information to consider about their health and lifestyles, as well as plans for the future and current challenges. As of September 2012, there were 53,364 centenarians in the US according to the U.S. Census Bureau. There are other country with large numbers of centenarians which include Brazil at 23,760; China at 17,800; United Kingdom at 11,600; France at 16,791; and Japan at 44,449.

Carmella Natale

Chapter 6: Faith

"That where there is doubt, I may bring faith"

The charming woman learns faith in the real self and the God within. St. Francis is remembered and preserved in history as a magnificent example of faith with all of its positive effects. It is possible to define doubt as the source of all illness. We humans make our reality through our beliefs all the time. When our faith is strong in something or someone, the results can be enormous. St. Francis lived by faith, and we're aware of his amazing life. He left a life of wealth as a merchant like his father and made a vow of poverty. He remained loyal to the church even though they were negative and non-supportive of him at times. He had great faith in his disciples, God, and nature.

This same power of faith is available to us, and can be used to bring us excellent health and normal body weight. Doubt, however, is one of the greatest problems in human life and can lead to illnesses or death. Doubt is like the cornerstone of the death belief system and is present in all limiting beliefs. The five limiting beliefs are: lack, limitation, loss, scarcity, and deprivation. These five are all aspects of the basic belief of the ego in destruction. The body is harmed and eventually destroyed by these beliefs.

It is therefore important to become aware of any doubt in our beliefs and thoughts. We can undo the detrimental vibe through faith and love. The ideal of total love for ourselves removes doubt and fears, raises our consciousness, increases our vibration rates, and improves our health. Body weight must follow the instructions of our minds and beliefs. Maintaining faith in the eventual achievement is the required daily discipline. Welcome to your new world of ideal body weight when love and faith are practiced daily in this way. Faith will find and select the very best diet and consume it daily.

Chapter 7: Hope

"That where there is despair, I may bring hope"

The charming woman brings hope in the power of love. Despair is one of ego's most prized achievements. It is a symbol of successful attack on Divine Love and perpetuates illusions that love does not exist at all or that it is reduced in value and effect to whatever degree it can be reduced in any situation. One of the favorite statements of despair is, "I love you, but..." During these times obesity is rampant, even in children, and despair is the cause and effect of being overweight. The desperation some obese people feel can be seen in the enormous increase in lap band surgery as the remedy for obesity. There are now many persons who joyfully give their testimonies about their return to being normal weight through the method, and they are very grateful for no longer being in despair.

The origins of despair are bought to fruition by the faith individuals express in illusions and fear. The value of changing from doubt to faith applies in many other areas, and it's easy to see how these beliefs are sources of despair. The importance of changing despair into hope cannot be overemphasized nor practiced too much or too often.

It is interesting and paradoxical to observe how dieting has become associated with despair. As stated earlier, "Diets don't work." This statement is the background for endless despair for many people. This subject is so vast and important that Sondra Ray entitled her book on weight as <u>The Only Diet There Is</u>, and her approach is essentially deciding to love oneself, learning how to do so and holding firm once there. The reduction in weight follows naturally as night follows day according to Sondra Ray, and she has many testimonies to support her approach.

    Hope is available in many forms and ways, and can be chosen at any moment as on decides to heal and release despair. When love and faith are present and functioning, hope is possible, realistic, and helpful. Safe weight then becomes a reality.

Chapter 8: Light

"That were there are shadows, I may bring light."

The charming woman illuminates the darkness and eliminates the shadows. Shadows can be defined as any energy interfering with having love and light to be fully present and expressed. All fears and all illusions can be equated with shadows. Dr. Carl G. Jung, the famous Swiss psychiatrist, brought the concept of the shadow into his practice and used it to help people transform their negatives into positives, fears into love, and darkness and shadows into light.

The traumatic experiences which people have throughout human history concerning food, maintaining the body and life are beyond problematic. Obesity is now being called an "epidemic" and other eating disorders abound. Shadows have played a central role in all of these problems, and fear is a shadow sometimes disguised as the real light of the Divine. Guilt is the shadow of judgment, casting a veil of obstruction which prevents perception of Light and clarity about Light and Dark. The five limiting beliefs which again are lack, limitation, loss, scarcity, and deprivation cast shadows, prevent total perception and clarity of the Light. St. Francis taught us to bring these shadows to the Light and love allowing them to be transformed through the healing process. The most effective way to establish this begins with complete honesty with self and admitting the problem. This step is also known as bringing a shadow to light.

The next important step is love, and learning to love the negative emotions and thoughts holding you back. At that point, you can channel and change any emotions and direct thoughts towards to positive outcome being sought.

Have you ever thought about the fact that food requires light for growth and maturation? The harvesting of food before it's fully ripe remains a matter of concern in our modern lifestyles. We are all eating some foods that were harvested before they had received enough light. If we buy fruit or vegetables that are not yet fully ripe and ready for use as food, what do we do? We place them where they can receive more light and leave them there until they are fully ripened. Isn't a paradox that food is digested in physical darkness? The energy of light is present in the cell and enters the cell as God's nourishment. When it is accompanied by love, we are properly and fully nourished. Even hard core science and conservative scientists are accepting that Vitamin D3 deficiency is one cause of cancer. The most common source of this vitamin is the Sun, the greatest source of Light in the material world.

Chapter 9: Joy

"That where there is sadness, I may bring joy"

The charming woman smiles often in private and public. Historically joy has been regarded as the ideal state of being and consciousness in which we are to live. When the shadows are transformed and love is continuously our state of mind and heart, joy is the natural result. In the prayer of St. Francis, the polar opposite is sadness. Sadness is a result of the five negative limiting beliefs which follows the experience of loss. Thus joy follows experiences of being whole, living in prosperity, freedom, and abundance. When humanity comes to the realization that we are to have joy as God has and gives joy, then we'll no longer have our bodies as barriers to our happiness. The clearest and most powerful statement of all demonstrated in the life of Jesus reads, "The Father and I are One." Because we're all connected and sons and daughters of the Most High God, the Father is One with ALL of us, and He loves us enough to send the Holy Spirit to be our guide.

The first statement of this book is, "When we are One with the One—God's Love, we inevitably win and triumph." Now we add, joy is our experience and constant reality. The shadows are transformed, and love is all there is…joy is present here and now. The past is transformed, completed, and cannot touch us. The soul is all about wisdom from all experiences. Upon transformation and complete atonement the loving thoughts and acts of love are the essence of our memories. Joy becomes the essence of our lives in the present.

The history of humanity can be seen as a piece of artwork which features billions of fragments of God. Each fragment believes that it's separate from the next and forever isolated from the Divine Creator, until they awaken. Once awakened, they remember who they really are, who created them, how, and why. They realize that the Divine is looking at the bigger beautiful picture, in which, they cannot see because they're part of it. Realizing it takes all of them to work together in harmony to show the beauty of gratitude to our Divine Creator by the contribution to peace. They become joyful, and joy becomes a perpetual reality. Literature and the arts have presented this image many times and in many ways. The theme is always the undoing of the belief in separation, the awakening to the real self, and the acceptance of our oneness with the One.

One of the most influential impacts of joy in history was created by Ludwig von Beethoven. His "Ninth Symphony" is regarded by many as his greatest work, and to some the most universal composition in the history of music. "Ode to Joy" is the title of the last part of the symphony, and sometimes it's also referred to as "The Symphony of Joy". People generally report a feeling of joy or more joy as they experience the musical ballad. The story of Beethoven becomes enriching as we discover he overcame serious challenges in his life. The decline in his hearing and eventual total deafness was a source of sadness, yet he retained joy. Because of that joy he continued to compose and work with music though he could not hear. An amazing part of the story of "Ode to Joy" is that as the premier opening concert was in progress, the audience exploded into thundering appreciative applause as the music reached the great crescendo. Beethoven was urged to turn and face the audience. He could see and experience the overwhelming applause, but he could hear nothing. What a mixture of joy and sadness, what a melding of blessings and losses. Think again of the peace and joy St. Francis experienced as the Pope said, "This man in his poverty has put all of us to shame," but at the same moment he felt the sadness of being unsupported in his life and work by his superiors. Stephan A. Levine put it this way, "The more sorrow that is carved into your heart, the more joy it can contain". Weight loss through love can be your "Ode to Joy".

Johann Sebastian Back made his great contribution to joy through his music, and one of his compositions is "Jesu, Joy of Man's Desiring". This beautiful piece is a classic, generates feelings and states of joy as it is experienced, and millions of humans have increased the joy in their lives through it. An interesting part of the story of this song has been the tendency of some performers to play it slowly, more in the form of a funeral dirge than one of sparkle and joyfulness. One performer states that the way Bach wrote the original was in the faster tempo, much more in tune with joy. This music is wonderful to include in the daily regimen for weight loss.

Carmella Natale

Chapter 10: Comfort

"Lord, grant that I may seek rather to comfort than to be comforted"

Food and the process of eating become very comforting, and is a relationship experienced from birth. Our first experiences in life include milk from the comforting breast of a mother's body or from a bottle with a soft comforting rubber nozzle. There are many stories of human infants whom weren't able to have the basic experience of comfort through food, and the results of this lack ranges from temporary discomfort to death. As a race of beings, we have generally regarded a perfectly nurturing infancy as a birthright, and this right is the best possible nutritional start in life.

As we move to adolescence and adulthood, the use of food in terms of comfort moves into importance in different ways. Excessive weight, obesity, diabetes and heart disease have become epidemic. Comfort food has become discomfort food for a portion of our population. The usual pleasures of eating our foods have become irritating and anxiety provoking; traveling full speed to a torture chamber. Worrying about calories, allergies, and other illnesses can make mealtime the most dreaded part of the day.

How did we get into such a state of difficulties with one of life's most basic and comforting daily experiences? There are now more excellent books, videos, and advice for help with diets and exercise than any one person can read or do. I desire to be truthful and simple. I truly believe based on my 93 years of experience, which includes owning an Italian restaurant, that the central factor is the real self versus the false self. When we believe that our real

God self within does not exist, or that we're separated from the inner Divine, **HUNGER** is created and will become gluttony, if not bought to a halt. The premise of this whole book is to change your thinking is to change your life. We must remember to carefully watch our thoughts, how we think about those thoughts, and finally what we say. Words have power." Thoughts become words, become actions, become you" is an old proverb and the meaning transcends any subject we can possibly imagine. It is especially true as it pertains to food and health.

Of course, our human tendency is to perceive the problem as only physical and perceive proper diet as the solution, but these are merely effects of a root cause. The cause is spiritual imbalance, which radiates outward into our actions. Things going on in our lives, outside of us, are reflections of our thoughts and emotions. Be open minded and do not consider proper diet as the only option or solution. How many individuals have lost excess weight only to gain it back? True comfort is found when connection to the Source is found. When we accomplish this goal, our system of desires change. In states of divine inner peace there is no spiritual hunger, and the body will follow suit wanting only natural foods in perfect amounts with joy during meals. Once we've achieved this state of being we can be what St. Francis envisioned: fully comforted and able to comfort others rather than seeking comfort for ourselves. Constantly seeking comfort for ourselves is disguised as hunger for the Divine and union with God.

Chapter 11: Understanding

"More to understand than to be understood"

St. Francis requests of the Divine that he be more mature, wise, and understanding in his relationships with his fellow human beings. These traits develop and are maintained through very challenging experiences, in which the discrimination of illusions from the reality of love is achieved. The history of humanity is blessed with the lives of many masters who passed the tests and transformed trials into blessings and laboratories for growth. St. Francis was certainly one of the masters, and founded an order to help people with leprosy. This order was devoted to the protection, welfare and improvement of life for the poor. He practiced love and understanding for everyone to the best of his ability. There were times when his superiors in the church did not understand him, but he found the strength to understand them in spite of the difficulties. His love and understanding was so powerful that we are aware of him and his accomplishments now and perhaps for all eternity.

When we apply this principle to the challenge of ideal body weight, it is easy to see that understanding of oneself and others is of great value in caring for one's body. When decisions about food and nourishment are guided by mature understanding, the problems of overweight are greatly reduced or even eliminated altogether. Understanding is capable of transforming all destructive thoughts and despair. The perceived needs and beliefs about self-protection can be changed through understanding. The practice of eating excessively in order to feel safe can be altered through understanding. Excesses, extremes and addictions can be laid aside as genuine love for the real self is achieved and practiced.

Chapter 12: Service

"For it is by self-forgetting that one finds love."

Jesus taught that loving others, therefore serving others is the ultimate will of God. "Whoever wants to become great among you must be your servant, and whoever wants to be first must be slave of all. For even the Son of Man did not come to be served, but to serve, and to give his life as a ransom for many." (Mark 10: 43-45) He then continues on as stated in John 13: 34 "A new command I give you: Love one another. As I have loved you, so you must love one another." According to the teachings of Jesus, the smallest act of service to anyone, especially a child, is the greatest decision one can make. St. Francis accepted all of these things and left a legacy of service with provides many different services to countless numbers of people all over the world daily. Miracles are done by those who temporarily have more for those who temporarily have less. St. Francis served the sick, poor, and unhappy. He also supported those who served others in whatever ways he could in his day and time.

The principles of love and service apply totally to the realms of food, health, and caretaking of our bodies. Abundance is the inherent basic nature of creation, earth, and universes. Service is totally vital to earth and all humanity because services are the delivery vehicles of all abundances that are available. There is more than enough love and food for everyone on earth, but service and delivery are required for everyone to benefit. We can all be inspired by Amma Chi of India who constantly shares her abundant supplies of love, food, and clothing. After the tsunami in India, she shared twenty million dollars with the affected families and the geographical areas injured by the huge waves. Her devotion to others in service in that situation as well as the endless, countless other situations of rendered service throughout her amazing life of service give us a model in expansive sizes of what we are to do all of the time, regardless of size or extent. Jesus taught and confirmed that the "smallest act of service" is equal to all service, and is the will of the Divine. Many wounds in need of healing are taken care of by the rendering of service. We do it for the Divine and to the Divine, however small or insignificant it may seem. When we are healed in these ways we are happier. Our body weight reveals a reflection of that peace and comfort if we so choose. It is of interest to note that Amma Chi herself carries some excessive weight. It's also interesting to observe that weight loss coaches and doctors who help people lose weight report that their vocations are very satisfying through the services they render to others. Losing weight through love is a "win-win" choice and process for everyone involved.

Chapter 13: Forgiveness

"For it is by forgiving that one is forgiven."

    The charming woman forgives. Most of us have deep wounds in our minds, hearts, and souls because we feel worthy only through suffering. Sometimes it seems guilt and misery are all that we know. Our perception is distorted. The light and peace in our lives is dimmed by shadows of doubt and corruption. Corruption is the misunderstanding of seeing today with the vision of the past, or past experiences instead of viewing the reality of unconditional love. The ugly sights of unresolved consequences make us want to shrink and silently disappear. Instead, we find comfort in food's nourishment and stuff our feelings and emotions by eating. Instead of shrinking we grow too large through too many unburned calories. We become more miserable.

    After coming to IL Sorentos in 1972, I was introduced to books about spirituality. Through my reading I came to understand that I was created as perfect love and also that I am perfectly loved. I reached a place where the things others did or said could not take the feeling of love away from me.

    Temptation is mental inertia asserting its survival. As we yield, guilt consumes us, and we express it as self-hatred instead of love. We remain in a state of being unforgiving. Awareness is our unconscious thought brought to the light of spiritual reality. Fantasy tempts us to freeze and do nothing. Thus, a favorite statement of mine from <u>A Course in Miracles</u> is: *"Forgiveness is the key to happiness. Forgiveness offers everything I want."* Therefore, what I want is my ideal weight and the best possible health in my body. Forgiveness brings it to me and you.

We must change our minds and realize that God's love is constantly our companion instead of being afraid of solitude. Without emotional response, our desires slip away and diminish. Pray to see God's Love and forgive yourself and all others completely. Pray to know and feel you deserve the best and good in life. The best and good include the best possible health and weight.

Since the problem is not outside of us or unresolved from the past, we may learn to depend on God. When we are able to break our unconscious identification within, we may become able to observe the pain, realize the cause, and stop feeding the issue by eating, fault finding, or attacking someone else. When I realized that my choice was to run away an feed my compulsion, I also realized I was making it stronger. Awareness is the energy and capability of triumph.

As we follow the healing process, we change behavior. In admitting our weakness we are blessed by God. A disciple follows direction, and we become strong and disciplined. Navigating through the paths of life we feast on God's love and follow Divine direction. Our pain diminishes when we usher in the process of not judging ourselves or others. A judgment is made whenever you compare yourself with another human being, or they compare themselves with you.

Forgiveness comes from awareness of the false self. Once we are aware of the false self, we don't need to attack ourselves or others. We are not naturally miserable people. We are created by God in the image and likeness of God.

I was living a nightmare running and seldom seeking beautiful ideas. The dull ache in my stomach that I perceived as hunger was spiritual starvation and deprivation. I ran in the shadows because the light was too bright. The veil of ignorance covered me where I experienced misery all of the time. Step from the shadows into the light. Resistance aches. Put on the light. Radiate the Divine. Stop…Look…*Feel.*

The more soul we express, the more beautiful we become. If we consider practicing a discipline that comes from unconditional love for thirty days, we will invariably find new habits forming. Unconscious repetition happens when we repeat false action so many times it becomes a habit. Today we awake with the resolve and ask for God's help.

One day I went with a friend to a prominent mall in Dallas for a sweet snack breakfast and attended the Arts Festival only to have a lunch laden with fats. The rich foods we delicious and delusion swept me into thinking I needed more. For three days, I binged on all my favorite fat foods and this demonstrated what I know now as unconscious repetition. I became full of pain instead of embracing the full love of God which was needed to satisfy my hunger.

Clearing is a cleansing process. We wash away negative thoughts and behavior, just as we wash food from our dishes. We demonstrate definite determined action and detoxify our mind. Anything that appears a problem is an illusion because we realize that everything that happens to us we've attracted to us. We ask for it. Forgiveness is seeing other people like God sees them *"Forgive them for they know not what they do."* (Luke 23:34 (NIV)) Everything is subjective belief, and it unfolds in our lives from our minds. The reason certain areas in our lives haven't changed is because we have not accepted the spiritual law involving that area.

God manifests through His heavenly and earthly angels. Sometimes these messengers bring us new ideas or thoughts. <u>A Course in Miracles</u> teaches us that miracles are corrections for our old thoughts and a shift to the loving thoughts of the fruits of the spirit. *"The fruit of the Spirit is love, joy, peace, forbearance, kindness, goodness, faithfulness, gentleness and self-control. Against such things there is no law."* (Galatians 5:23 (NIV))

Our old thoughts are judgments of ourselves and others. Thoughts like: *I don't deserve to be happy; I am fat and ugly: I don't deserve to be blessed; Why can they do something and I can't.* That's the voice of our false self speaking. It is suggested that we not reinforce those kinds of thoughts because they grow and multiply. Instead we should simply smile, stop, and consider the source and the cost of the negative thought. Stand back and observe yourself. We are sons and daughters of God.

We reinforce the illusion when we react to the pain from our thoughts by feeding it with food; instead of dealing with it and acknowledging the root cause. Any continuing pattern of reaction makes the pain more real and intense. The more we talk about it, the more real we make it.

When unconscious desire takes over, our false self dulls our senses and stores the thoughts and emotions we ignore, as fat cells. We lack conscious thought and perceive an absence of nourishment. Our false self indulges in the folly of devouring doughnuts or demanding instant satisfaction from fatty foods. We are falsely nourished and stay hungry. Once we become aware of our false self and choose to change it, we actively acknowledge the ego and accept our real self, our Godly self.

Chapter 14: Awakening

"It is by dying that one awakens to Eternal Life."

The charming woman allows the death and burial of the false self. She becomes aware of her real self, or Godly and Divine inner self. The real self has it's reality in love, faith, hope, joy, happiness, sharing, and beauty; all the positive traits of the fruits of the Spirit as stated in Galatians 5:23 and by St. Francis. Release any despair or self criticism you may have within your thoughts. The journey and arrival are one, and I assure you it's worth its weight in gold. Reading and practicing the principles in this book are rewarding in themselves.

One of the best books I know concerning awakening was written by one of the most spiritually evolved people on Earth, Stephen A. Levine. A gradual awakening is also a gentle awakening with Stephen's guidance. He describes how hurts, defenses and the deadening of ourselves have happened and the results which have manifested. He offers a loving, gentle path to becoming fully alive and awake again.

In the first several chapters of one of his books, Stephen describes the human ego, its defenses, and shows how defenses can make us "sleepwalkers". We're less awake and aware than we can and need to be. He describes denial, depression, fear, and all forms of unforgiveness as the cause s of our being less aware and living in captivity of our own thoughts, emotions, and beliefs. This perspective is also biblical according to Galatians 5:13-26

It is of importance to know that when Stephen Leving met Ondrea, his life partner of many years, she had cancer. They decided to heal her through meditation, love, and other things know to assist in healing cancer. Nine months were required and they succeeded. Stephen and Ondrea have lived to gether as a phenomenal relationship ever since.

As we have seen in previous chapters, pain relief can become the main goal of existence leading to drugs, alcohol, and food. These addictions disguised as pain relief become the tranquilizers used to reduce pain or negative thinking. The false self becomes stronger as we live and become accustomed to holding negative thoughts and pain. The need for awakening to the real self becomes acute. A crisis can become necessary to open the processes of healing through forgiving others and ourselves. There are feelings of dread and fear, as we start answering the great question: "Who are we, really?" Reluctantly, we enter the process of awakening and allow our real self to emerge. The dominance of the false self subsides, and we realize that we are more than conquerors when attuned to the inner divine love of God radiating from the inside out.

The following exercise serves as an example which will prove helpful when done consistently over a period of time. It will lead to a complete change from the false self to the real self.

> Step 1: Think of someone you feel has hurt you or someone in which you have hurt. Consciously choose now to love them rather than judge or condemn them by sending positive thoughts as you visualize them in your mind.
>
> Step 2: While holding them in your visualization, say to them, "I choose to perceive only the positive, only the good, only the God consciousness in you."
>
> Step3: Now say to them, "God is the love in which I forgive you

Step 4: Hold yourself in your visualization in your conscious and only see the good choosing to release all judgment and negative thoughts or feelings against yourself. Say to yourself now, "God is the love in which I forgive myself."

Step 5: Say now, "In my defenselessness my safety lies."

You can sense how powerful this process is and how powerful it can be for you if you practice regularly and consistently. No limits are present here because it's a process that develops over days, weeks, or maybe years.

Carmella Natale

Chapter 15: Apply Psalm 91 and Transform Guilt

Psalm 91: 14-16
> *"Because He hath set His love upon me, I will deliver him. I will be with him in troubles. I will deliver him and honor him with long life. I will satisfy him."*

Illusions seem to separate us from God's love bringing feelings of isolation and drawing us away from our real self. Ego attacks an hour after a snack, disguising itself as hunger. Beware of the ego's isolation. Separation from attunement with the inner Divine keeps us in deprivation and we starve.

Create a new picture. Let's see ourselves supplied and satisfied as God sees us. Let us be willing to become aware because we are full with God. Compulsive eating demonstrates lack and reflects that we don't feel God's love. Evidence of the false self manifests as we repetitively demand more. Seemingly feelings and thoughts of endless guilt are the reward for making and accepting the illusions as our reality. We have attacked ourselves with our own ego.

How do we regain peace of mind, deep inner calm, and lasting states of satisfaction? We do this by avoiding judgments of all kinds, false interpretations and illusions. We ignore pointing fingers which in the end only shame us into feelings of guilt and anger. When another person points a finger, they're asking for God's love. Hear them asking, "Love me please!"

Stop…Look…Ask, "Is there any TRUTH in this bite, any true taste for me?" God pays us a generous allowance of peace, love, acceptance, and forgiveness. This allowance creates space for more calm and less chaos. God's love satisfies and fills us full unto overflowing.

Compulsion is corruption. By eating compulsively we put off our natural dominion over the challenge we avoid. Guilt is the inevitable result of affirming the illusion as real insists, it's Instead, let us claim and affirm with all our being:

"I am cherished by God. I am loved unconditionally and totally."

Carmella Natale

www.ingramcontent.com/pod-product-compliance
Lightning Source LLC
Chambersburg PA
CBHW050508120526
44588CB00044B/1797